THE **DEVIL** IS A SKILLED VENTRILOQUIST

MARISA CRANE

PROMENADE
PRESS

THE DEVIL IS A SKILLED VENTRILOQUIST
WRITTEN BY MARISA CRANE
ALL RIGHTS RESERVED

COVER ART AND DESIGN BY MATTHEW HENSON
EDITED BY FRANCES VEGA

COPYRIGHT 2017 © PROMENADE PRESS, LLP
WWW.PROMENADE-PRESS.COM

THE DEVIL IS A SKILLED VENTRILOQUIST

MARISA CRANE

If You See Her

Tell her the air never lost its thickness.
The guillotine is rusting in the town square
waiting to try me for my sins.

If you see her,
tell her the wine is still here.
It's been eight years
and I just learned
that wine doesn't better with age.
It regresses into a grapevine
you use to hear about my that embodies my latest love,
tangled but unbreakable.

Tell her I have scars along my spine
hundreds of years older than me.
Centuries of rebirth have taught me
to romanticize destruction.

The wrong me showed up with her.
It feels as if
I have written this poem
a thousand times
before documenting its truth.

If you see her,
tell her it's hard to wake up
feeling rested
when I spend all night
tracing the nine circles of hell
eventually swallowing the flames
surrounding each ring.

I'm jealous of the stars.
They emit more beauty
while dead
than I ever have alive.
Breathing isn't so easy
and dying isn't so hard.

I do it every day that I wake up
and she is not here,
wondering in which century
I lost my heart.

Coffin

It's 3 AM
and your side of the bed
is no longer yours to miss.
The air is cold like a sweat
I didn't work for,
and the winds are untamed
like this pulse I can't constrain.
You are denting
someone else's mattress
and stealing forever's
off someone else's choir tongue.

I am sifting through
old photographs and love letters
I collected,
like vices you didn't have to fear,
and I never realized
this shoebox I revere
is starting to look more like
an infant's coffin
than a time capsule
you never bothered to exhume.

The drinks flow easily
as the darkness slips into gray.
I don't care if the glass
is half empty or half full.
Either way,
I'm going to drink it down
to the burning core of the earth
and wait until I feel
anything other than "just okay."

It's 5 AM
and your face is seared in my mind -
the crooked curve of your smile,
the ineffable warmth of your eyes.
Your asymmetrical dimples

7

dressed as contagions for my soul.
The face of a woman
who thought I was enough,
who was deluded into thinking
I was enough.

After so many
Weathervanes left me
unaware of where I belong,
I've come to understand
that the only real litmus test for love
is wishing for someone's happiness
and truly meaning it,
regardless of the circumstances,
regardless of the collateral heartache.

All of Me

Long distance call -
I accept
this slow dance with death.

I know you know
I still struggle
with my times tables
(No matter the equation,
the product was never you),
and I still grapple
with this arms race
(Mine always come up empty).

I am tired
of dropping quarters
into phones
and hearing voices beg
for the whole of me.
This hole in my chest
knows no symmetry,
knows no translation
for the metaphors
I scribble on bar napkins.

I was never able to say this before
so I'm saying it now:

I'm sorry ...
"Your call has run out of time.
If you wish to stay on the line,
please add more coins."

Click.

Stinger

Some mornings I wake
still searching for my stinger.
How frantic,
how senile,
I must be,
to feel nostalgia
for the worst part of me.
I wonder where it has gone
and who fashions it now,
if they turn it on themselves
just as I once did.

I'd only wanted confirmation
that I was real.
I'd only wanted to trace
the striations of you,
the ones that resembled my stripes;
I've long since blended
into palatable hues.

We could have slipped
into darkness
and held each other
if we'd desired,
but I think
we were already doing that:
holding each other back
because we wanted

so we couldn't
sting ourselves
anymore.

Omission

Maybe
we can't be
the Us
we always thought
we could be...

but an ellipsis
fashioned from abandoned dreams
and death's own fears.

It leaves our love wondering
whether it was ever
up to us
in the first place.

Forgetting Was Never an Option

I remember it.
I remember it
because it hurt.
Looking at you
looking at her,
through a kaleidoscope of wonder.
Me?
I searched through
underwater caves
and snagged my limbs
on coral reefs.
My searing blood swam
while our stale contraband sank.

What is it about newness,
the virgin love that floats
through a tinted rain
and intoxicates our palms?
Your cigarette fingers
light naked nerve endings
of another,
while I'm left to be put out
prematurely.

I've seen the afterlife,
French kissed heathens
and held angels up at gun point.
Nothing compares
to the night of inexplicable
goodbyes
and deserted promises.

I'm convinced the Devil
must be a skilled ventriloquist,
throwing his cold rejections
into the mouths of lovers
as he sits back
and smokes a joint

to the sound of crystalline hearts
shattering.

Believe me,
when I said loving is unbearable,
it was you I had in mind,
and when I said
I won't recover from this,
it was my soul
you'd chosen to suck out.

Torn Out

These are the journal entries we revisit,
the feelings we can't believe were ever real.

Sometimes I'm too in love with you to speak.
I don't really believe in a lot of things,
but I think this is it for me.
I think you're it.

Who were we when we wrote these things
and did we know we'd bury them before long?
Did we know the words would soon become possessed
by the world conspiring against us?

Screw you for ruining the best thing
that's ever happened to either of us.
I can't get up in the morning knowing I don't have you.

I sit and think,
sift and drink,
and eventually,
I tear you from this notebook
like it's the only place you've ever lived.

These are the obituaries
of which no one ever speaks.

Lying In Pools of Our Own Blood

This is the pipe
we stuff full of strife
and animosity.
This is the pipe we light
on eternity's eve,
as we inhale the smoke
from tantalizing fights.

Have you ever seen War
slip into a sundress
and knock on her neighbor's door,
colorblind
and beckoning like a silent film?

She examines the world
over tea
and need not have her pinky out
for everyone to know her prestige.

Tell me,
what were monsters called
before we gave them a name?
Were they as phantasmic
as our moonlit metaphors?
Did they slur
like my guttural, drunken pleas
outside your dorm room window?
You always told me
those nights never seemed
to go to bed
and at the time
I considered the possibility
that love has never known
even a sliver of my essence.

War brews inside our heads,
bubbling over like an ill poured beer.
It's a tumor swallowing our matter

and sharpening its knives
while we struggle to eat with our hands.

This crimson anguish,
buried at the core of my DNA,
is an infinite, spiral staircase
and I am forever vomiting
over the railing.

This is the pipe
we stuff full of regret
and mourning.
This is the pipe we light
on compassion's grave
as we inhale the smoke
from too many casualties
and not enough empathy.

How is it
that we can claim to be alive
when we breathe in poisons
the rest of the universe
seems to have never heard of?

Open Casket

Open casket,
open hearts,
quivering knees find sadness
to kneel on
and worship a bloodied Jesus,
while I refuse to worship
anyone but you.
My tears taste
of your late-night laughter,
that I loved to indulge in so much.
That smile held me in one hand
and a lust for discovery
in the other.

This is not a love story,
it is a broken story,
and it is mine to carry.
I walk facing the misery
you left behind.
I embrace the man
you grew to resemble
so profoundly
and I love him
for his love,
for his reigning words.

"Oh sweetheart,
you know he would have
dropped everything
and married you, baby."

Now I'm the sobbing widow
of unrequited love.

Fire

The night was wet with liquor
and I was drinking myself
back to life,
back to worth,
back to surgical grace,
and savored days.
You'd been charred by a love
unrequited
yet sometimes feigned at 2 AM.
Afterward,
you'd always hold me
like a polaroid
you didn't want to smudge,
but even with your delicate care,
I never allowed my love
to properly develop.

I couldn't help but wonder
if I'd have looked better
blurry and out of focus.

I remember smoking
on the third floor balcony,
your voice piercing
our underwater world,
*"the rain will always fall,
won't it?"*
Yes,
but it's okay to be rain,
love,
it's okay to be rain.
Bilingual monsters
translated your fears for me.
*"Dear,
I think he'd rather be the flames."*

That was the night
your fist met forbidden glass

18

and I was the only one
who could smell the smoke-
the only one who understood
there was a fire that needed
extinguishing.

The Art of Leaving

Throat like a gutter,
my stray cries reverberate,
but no one stops.

There goes another love poem
dead on arrival.

This tunneling is joyless,
this fucking isn't a prescription,
it isn't smoking opium on a porch
or performing an exorcism.

I don't know what to call it.

Perhaps pantomimed closure
or improvised seduction?

Whatever it is,
it must be relinquished.

If you see me wandering the streets,
it's because I lost my keys last night
hopping from incubus to incubus.

I hear there are cliffs
overlooking the sea
with graffiti talking of
dismemberment and love,
and how you couldn't be
any closer to you
and I couldn't be
any further from me.

Death March

You have long since buried
the abstract notion,
the brilliant future of us
(I've meant to as well,
believe me,
but that requires a strength
I've yet to build).
It was methodical
the way you lifted the dirt
onto our carcass,
and it was methodical
the way your gaze
said goodbye each day
before you'd even left me.

It's been many suns;
piano keys grew from the soil
this past spring
and I couldn't find middle C,
but I played you a death march
nonetheless.

You've left me innumerous voicemails
with explicit instructions,
and yes,
I know the shovel
is leaning against the shed
where I used to store my feverish dreams.

I'll get to it someday.
It's just that today
your ghost makes
an excellent dance partner.

On Distance

What time is it where you are?
It's mid-morning here
and I'd prefer to remain anonymous.
I don't wear suffering so well -
Not like a flowing gown,
not like a nude body,
I actually feel comfortable in.

I hope you can smell
the rain today.
It's been hazy here as well.
People's eyes look more tired than usual
and my jeans have gotten a bit loose.
The clocks sometimes run backwards
on their heels,
tripping over themselves,
and the ticking keeps me up most nights.

Before today I never thought it possible
that two people in the same room
could reside in different time zones,
but I promise you that they can.

You and I,
we make it look easy,
but certainly not good.

The Absurd

I want to ask her
what she thinks about absurdism,
but she is toying
with the idea of leaving
and that question
might push her over the edge.

Instead,
I will open a new bottle
and not assign value
to anything at all,
because I can't be an alcoholic
without a label
and she can't be leaving
without a vantage point.

Later I will lie in bed,
memorializing senseless love,
and wonder how it is I stay alive
with the hearse honking outside
my bedroom window
every night.

November

I remember the November rain
and the way it painted our skin,
rambling prose skipping like stones.
I remember straddling your hips
and covering your chest in stamps
as if your heart hadn't already
been sent away
(I think a sliver of me still hoped
you'd written a return address).
I remember learning
what a smile looks like
when someone is falling out of love
and searching your medicine cabinet
for something else to blame.

Maybe you remember it all too.
Maybe you check the mailbox each day
for a bomb activated by love.
Maybe you tell anyone who will listen
that you hate the rain
and that your smile
has always been crooked.

Maybe you don't
think of me at all
until you read this.

Yesterday

I wish the saber-toothed sadness
would keep it down;
I'm trying to sleep.
Our old friend Yesterday is back
and he's playing violin in the corner
like he never needed lessons
in the first place.
I'm lying in crop circles
made by his pointer finger,
reminders of his insistence that we're always alone,
no matter what we do.

But isn't this what we've been doing
all along?
Lying to ourselves
and everyone around us,
claiming we've had visitors
who care enough
to leave evidence
of their presence behind?

Apothecary

It's a turbulent Tuesday evening,
and I trek to the liquor store
to replenish my parched blood.

Cashier by the name of Josh
smiles like his puppeteer
passed out holding the strings
tied to the corners of his mouth.
Does he know that he doubles
as an apothecary,
doling out cures
to anyone with a 10 to spare
and a throat to burn?

I dip a bucket
into the well of swanned sadness
and come up empty-handed.
I can't possibly rid myself
of a despair
adorned with your silver ions
and donning your midnight glasses
that I swear let you see through
all the welled-up madness.

Got your initials tattooed
on the inside of my wrist today
(How laughable any other pain is
after your best friend dies),
and you were the first one
I wanted to show.

Written in script
for the man
that refused to treat life
as if he were reading from one.

Most people -
nothing more than stars

in their own little shows,
forget their lines
and sleep with the understudies.

Exit stage right.

I'd rather a perpetual loop
of nothingness
on a glistening,
shadowed stage
than anyone who thinks
they can give birth
to an everlasting light
that rivals
his phosphorescent truth.

Un-poem

Depression:

when even the words
I love you
sound like the morose slicing
of a guillotine.

Not Always Fortunate Fortunes
(Inspired by Frank O'Hara's "Lines for the Fortune Cookies")

You will collect vices like old photographs.

You will dream of shooting an apple off your lover's head, but upon waking, she will not let you try.

You will see love up close then it will gallop away.

You don't realize how many people admire you.

You will publish a book of poetry, and it will not be a best-seller.

You are not a Taurus like you'd always been led to believe.

You will fall for the Northern Lights in a lover's eyes.

Your mirror lies to you. You must learn to love your body.

You will write thousands of short stories and they will all be rejected.

That's not a devil on your shoulder. You just forgot to sleep.

Your words inspire others -sometimes to ruin themselves.

You will finish your first novel and waste money to print it just so you can throw it away.

You will move to the beach and forget the world.

You preach acceptance but your temper tends to distract you.

People will stare as you write this. Not everyone appreciates the arts.

You will publish a book that winds up being on the Banned Book List.

You will say you're happy and you will mean it.

Possessed

The Bible's only holy
because someone said it is.

Well,
I say it's holy
the way you sip
your champagne
and turn seconds into crystals
I can wear,
moments into icicles
I can compare
to a monster's teeth
in an enclosed cave.

I am not a revision.
I am not evolved
or advanced.
I am in my natural state
of living -
both fearless and frightened,
both volatile and steady,
both neurotic and sane,
both needy and distant.

I should have told you
long ago,
there is something in me
not yet named;

hand me a mask
and I'll lie to you
about lying
just to mime indifference
at the places where
fire and desert meet
most often.

You are walking
on the ceiling
showing off
your middle finger;

you are pretending
the sheep
notice your wounds,
bandaged yet still bleeding.

If Jesus could walk on water,
you could most certainly,
without claim,
without understanding,
walk all over me.

Inevitable

I'm thinking of the other night
and your hand on my leg.
I swear,
a bottle of beta blockers
couldn't have slowed my heart.

I'm thinking of all the things
that fill us up.
I'm staring at my palm full of electricity.
There's an energy between us
braided with gleaming giants
towering over unfinished cities.

Tell me I'm your tomorrow
and every day after.
Tell me I'm an atlas in your hands.
Tell me this craving for you
is insatiable,
and my intrepid tongue
will prove you right.

I'm thinking of the other night
and your lips on my neck.
I swear,
I felt them somewhere else.

I'm thinking of all the mirrors
that have lied to you
over the years.
I'd take centuries of bad luck
just to end their deceitful lives.

Tell me it's science
the way my pain
becomes your pain,
your emptiness -
my vacancy.
Transference of all that is

pure.

Tell me that
we won't miss out
on each other
and I'll tell you
that we're inevitable,
like the depths of your eyes.

Fast Blood

Night watch: the moon's capillaries
connect my idle handles to clarity.

My thighs host the memory
of you, the blood racing in a man-made heaven.

The black sky spies
on my eroded epiphanies.

Cannibal dreams spent deceiving and decadent -
violins incinerating at the end of the world.

I am collected like a valued trinket
from years ago, only to be revealed a replica.

This love is undoubtedly an anagram,
two hemispheres entwined.

Mine and yours and yours and mine;
a skilled ventriloquist the past is,
hurling its frozen lies through the window
and posing as a beggar dressed in dusk.

Glancing into your museum eyes,
I slowly thaw as I wait for admission.

Paradise

There is a heaven no one knows of.
It's void of promises and green pastures.
Harps don't play themselves
while the tipsy angels dream
lazily in ponds of white-lace bliss, simmering
in the shafts of light and streams,
cool like the other side of the pillow.

Except in this heaven
the pillows never warm - chilled and bound
by the love cells hurling through us - strangely
we don't question it, just dress
in our favorite nude skin
and dance off-beat. Stalling.
I read Carver to her,
"What We Talk About When We Talk About Love,"
so that I don't have to fumble over
the words we talk
yet don't talk
about.

Symptomatic

This morning was symptomatic.
Of what? I think I may know.
Serene. Fulfilled. Ethereal.
There's a sea of sheets,
and perhaps it is true
that I am not a strong swimmer,
born with a stubborn diffidence,
but at first light
she buoys my fortitude.

There was a pleasant breeze
she spoke of
as if she had dreamt it up herself.
When she speaks like that,
she asks if I am cold
due to the goose bumps
creeping up my arms.

I say yes even when I am not.

This morning was symptomatic.
She watched as I dressed for work.
I could see her eyes follow me
as if she were a contemporary
Mona Lisa,
only she didn't hide her teeth.

It's the simple things,
she said,
and I know exactly
what she means.

If

If you can still be inspired
by the way she sleeps
until noon,
untroubled by reality;
if you can still be enchanted
by the way the morning mist
outside your window
seems to sculpt
around her glass figure;
and if you can still be mystified
by her silhouetted lips,
reminiscent of exotic
and golden days,
drinking in the twilight's
seductive hues;
then you can,
without a doubt,
survive this turbulent
and civil warred life.

Worth

I am a work in progress
and you are a series of moments
shorter than scientists can measure
and faster than the sublime light you shed.

My brain laughs at itself
as the day's teeth marks
embroider my skin
and bruise my tough hide
(wish you were here).

I cartwheel into the sky.
I love how it looks just before it storms.
The sun throws punches
until the last round
and sweats through unblinking eyes.

And you want to know what else?
I love the smile on a child's face at Sea World
before he finds out the killer whales are abused,
the trusting moment before discovery.
I love the same kid that starts a petition
to save the whales,
the kid that packs it in his father's briefcase
and counts the signatures before bed every night.
The kid that learns how to mail a letter
and the worth of a stamp,
the worth of an animal's life.

When I smile into your eyes,
I am certain you were once that child.
Brooding in cool streams
of compassion and understanding,
you savor the succulent juices
of a heart ruptured open.
Through the thick smog
of my disaffected vessels,
you recognize my worth,

and with each kiss you transform
into a monument,
you ensure that I do
too.

After years of adoring snow days
while abhorring the snow,
it has occurred to me
that love is and always will be
about appreciating others
for who they are,
not for what they can do for you.

Hitchhiking

I am frigid
with fear
as you lie
on my shoulder
curling around
the night's sweet whisper
and kissing me
in the past tense.

I know that
I am not the one.

I know that you are
a long way from home.

Writer's Block

The sea's delectable breeze,
silk-woven - somber solitude.
The thing about this new orient,
I haven't been writing.
Sure, I've been writing
but not the way that I savor.
I can't pick out a single word
that isn't self-indulgent and pretentious,
the wither like flowers
that crave love
but dare not ask for it.
The well has run dry
and I scamper through drains,
picking at scraps I once rejected,
and sifting through my remains.
This cantankerous mind of mine
has discovered artifacts of me,
poorly-erected them,
and put them on display.
Free admission,
but please don't touch.
My vertebrae,
as you know,
have spikes for bones,
and no one can ever hold me
the way that they like,
can ever appreciate the bleeding
that comes if they do.

For now,
I will nurse this passion
and rock it to sleep.
It will be waiting a lifetime,
I'm afraid.

At the Source

Incredulous!
What unspeakable things happen
when you stop peering through microscopes
and begin to shrink your ego
and grow your time?

Swim down the source,
pray to bourbon gods
on life-stained knees -
bloodless yet persevering.
There are gritty teepees of bliss
on the rock next to me
and a songbird waterfall
on my other side -
amorphous,
depending on perspective,
translucent and present.

A portal to a better dimension
gives me fuck-me eyes
through its relinquishing branches.
Not ivory but ivory if she so desires.
My cells are
quarantined with absinthe brush
and liquid miracles
void of human charades,
succubi jumping up and down
on the suspension bridge
above me
who dare not come meet
the winding world
at its aching dawn.

Self-sabotage

Oh, sweet sacrifice, saccharine dreams
                of self-sabotage.
I begin with my shirt,
pull it over my head,
then my pants
                (I'm not wearing any underwear);
I unclip my bra.
Then I peel off my skin,
step out of it like a jumpsuit.
Rip out my hair,
set it on the windowsill
for the neighbors to admire.
                A potted plant of bloody knives
tips...
over the past decade
romance has been synonymous
with mutilation
and love may try her damnedest
to make casualties of us all
                but it's always my own hand
that makes the final cut.

Confessional

This morning,
my car is a confessional.
I'm right where you left me.
I can still taste the flames
from the hoops you made me jump through.
The burns on my chest and thighs
are starting to blister.
The tequila, though, the tequila
won't burn no matter how badly I want it to.
I lick the salt off the day's lower back -
she dons a sultry mist -
and wonder how much blood
I can trade for a lover that won't romanticize me.
Will the femoral artery do? Perhaps the carotid?
Where should I paint it if this pain has no door
and will the Angel of Death recognize
that my darkness is my first born?

I hope not.
I hope not.

Take it for slaughter;
I could use a break
from this anchored life for a while.

Birthday Party

I've got scars on my body
far older than me.
Did you hear me?
Far older,
far more tender.
I know I've fumbled through
this tangled play
countless times before,
but I can't seem to remember
which line follows your exit,
which delivery puts guns
in the throats of the audience
or which spectators to picture naked
(doesn't matter; I've seen them all).

And the cut-out sky, what of it?
Yesterday there was no sky,
and today I fall down its well,
lapping up regret
and lamenting my inability to improvise,
to veer from the ungodly script,
and tell you that I love you,
that I've always loved you,
and that tomorrow I shall die.

10,000 years old to the day.

Drag

Maybe she's an interpreter
of death.

Maybe.

Linguistic, levitating...
Reverberations paint this jail cell,
delectable like parables
whispered after a few too many beers.

>A woman once rescued a frozen snake
>from a storm,
>brought him inside and warmed him up.

He bit her, didn't he?
She died, didn't she?

>His tongue twitched with delight
>as he reminded her,
>"You knew I was a snake
>when you brought me in."

Dressed in drag,
we fool the world.

A Eulogy

There is a little girl
with light-up shoes
running down the street
to meet the ice cream truck,
fist clutching onto her cash.
She is grinning and her pigtails
whip her in the face.
She reaches the corner
where she has seen it stop before,
but it drives right on by.

Some deaths go unnoticed.
Some deaths happen in public.

Armor

I. There's a monster in the corner and she shares my DNA.
    Double helixes coded with icicles;
    crack it to find out what love is and is not.

Watch me fall apart.

II. The chains that hold her in place are short.
I know this because I measure them every day.

But today, the beast snakes closer.

Tremble with me.

III. Habituation. Lift glass. Swallow mercury. Fill glass. Repeat.
    I know you know when I'm rising.

IV. We missed out on each other, didn't we?
    Lie to me and tell me I'm a pretty little fool.
    Make me believe in you
    as I believe I'm 19 again.

V. Fear like armor. Hardened. Something I shine.

Creep closer. Obey the madness. There's plenty of room for two.

VI. Be soft, I warn.
But hearts make the most delectable guns.

VII. Retreat into the shell of myself,
    where I am safe, where I am warm,
    where nothing traumatic can happen.

But, nothing really happens in that shell, does it?

Guilty, As Always

On trial for my delusions.
I've created more than enough
alibis to escape from myself
for one lifetime.

This asphyxiated truth,
these disengaged ventricles -
sloppy and seeping.
Strokes of midnight
spent punching the clock
only to ice his bruises later
while I sober up with shitty coffee
and displaced emotions.

Silver tongues braid together
like our bodies used to do
on those warm, summer evenings
we thought we were
the first ones
to ever think of cheating death.

Take a shot of Jameson
and bury the life we could have shared
had the universe not gotten drunk
and changed our course.

Keep on Dancing

She lines up figurines
on her dresser,
and tries to figure out
what it means
to simultaneously
fear and covet love,
to have feelers
at the end of every vessel -
born from her heart
but numb to the touch.
Little glass girls
in dresses and hats
host clandestine meetings
with giants learning ballet.
A morning routine
like sex and coffee -
sugar, no cream.

The lesson is always the same -
if your world shatters,
keep on dancing.

One-way

How many times
do you have to jump
in front of a moving car
in your mind
before a part of you dies
in real life?

       Stop light synapses
       on a one-way street;
       everyone drives the wrong way.

I bet it's 12
because that's the number
I wear on my back like a bull's-eye.
The world never misses.

       Head-on collisions
       are like unwanted nuptials,
       we marry the agony
       simply because it's there.

Clinical
(A spoken word piece)

Sometimes it's hard to tell the difference
between a clinical condition and the human condition.
So quick to diagnose,
we forget volatility and melancholy
are appropriate responses
to a world that has fucked us
without our consent.

A therapist specializing in depression
will tell you you're depressed
while one with experience in trauma
will slap a PTSD label on you.

Me?
I wear this invisible name tag around
like I'm at a party no one invited me to.
Only at the end of the night,
I don't get to rip it off.
It tells me I'm crazy,
that I was put together improperly
by some drunken elf
brooding in the basement of the North Pole,
and I hold these parts together
with self-loathing as the glue -
I can't even huff it
on the days I'm feeling blue.

Sometimes it's hard to tell the difference
between a clinical condition and the human condition.
So accepting of every diagnosis,
we forget that numbness
might be the only way to cope
with a world that has fucked us
ten times over.
A world that once filled us with hope
then tipped our glass hearts back
and downed every last drop

until we became nothing more
than an empty vessel
guided by disappointment.

Sometimes we don't want to tell the difference
between a clinical condition and the human condition.
It's easier to assume
that intense emotions
are a result of a malfunction
instead of the norm -
That the rage people name hurricanes after
is a neurological disturbance,
that the sadness that sinks ships
is a chemical imbalance,
that unprecedented joy
should set alarms off in our heads.

Everything doesn't have to be clinical.
I am not a symptom of something greater.
I am me and some days
I am sad beyond comprehension,
others I am empty or bored,
while others I am manic
and dripping with imagination.

Sometimes I am tight-rope walking tears
and I don't know if they're flavored by
anger, joy, or despair,
and sometimes it doesn't matter,
because it's okay
to be every emotion
stuffed inside one person.

It is okay to not understand
why I feel what I feel.

The important thing is that I do.

All the Women Inside of Me

I am a Russian Nesting Doll
slicing myself at the waist each morning
(so no one will notice the cuts)
and emancipating all my former selves.

All the women inside me,
all the numb, paralyzed women;
they ache for a release,
and things like whiskey,
desolation, and a weathered notebook,
revive them.
There are antidotes I never meant to discover,
warm and familiar, like the sun
on the back of my neck,
while I streamline my romantic visions
and light candles in the park.

My former selves
are so attentive and needy-
baby ducks donning dresses
and rosy cheeks trailing behind me
wherever I go, wherever I stumble.
Whether it be on blind dates or job interviews,
they are never far behind,
but these aren't dolls
for the bright-eyed children.

Have you ever seen the films starring Chucky?
I wasn't always so nice, so soft,
so tragically sentimental.
In fact, sometimes my clones
(eager understudies sharing a spliff backstage)
step in for me when I am not looking,
when my insecurity slips a date rape drug
in my drink
and fucks me blind.

What shape do you take on

when you have no more bones to break?
Who do you become
when becoming was never the problem?

If only I could learn to stay.
I must be going now.

Goodbye.